Rhinoceroses

D1304254

Quinn M. Arnold

seedlings

CREATIVE EDUCATION • CREATIVE PAPERBACKS

Published by Creative Education and Creative Paperbacks
P.O. Box 227, Mankato, Minnesota 56002
Creative Education and Creative Paperbacks
are imprints of The Creative Company
www.thecreativecompany.us

Design by Ellen Huber; production by Joe Kahnke
Art direction by Rita Marshall
Printed in the United States of America

Photographs by Alamy (Barbara von Hoffmann, Tom Uhlman),
Corbis (Minden Pictures), Dreamstime (Gualtiero Boffi, Volodymyr
Byrdyak, Chat9780, Tibor Fazakas, Gvision, Iracha, Jonpym,
Kikikind, Mpetersheim, Leung Cho Pan, Jason Prince, Bernhard
Richter, Kaido Rummel, Tilo, Prapass Wannapinij), iStockphoto
(Anna Kucherova, S_Lew, Tsuji)

Library of Congress Cataloging-in-Publication Data
Arnold, Quinn M.
Rhinoceroses / Quinn M. Arnold.
p. cm. — (Seedlings)
Includes bibliographical references and index.
Summary: A kindergarten-level introduction to rhinoceroses,
covering their growth process, behaviors, the habitats they
call home, and such defining features as their horns.
ISBN 978-1-60818-797-3 (hardcover)
ISBN 978-1-62832-350-4 (pbk)
ISBN 978-1-56660-844-2 (eBook)
1. Rhinoceroses—Juvenile literature.
QL737.U63 A74 2016
599.66/8—dc23   2015041994
CCSS: RI.K.1, 2, 3, 4, 5, 6, 7;
RI.1.1, 2, 3, 4, 5, 6, 7; RF.K.1, 3; RF.1.1

First Edition HC 9 8 7 6 5 4 3 2 1
First Edition PBK 9 8 7 6 5 4 3 2 1

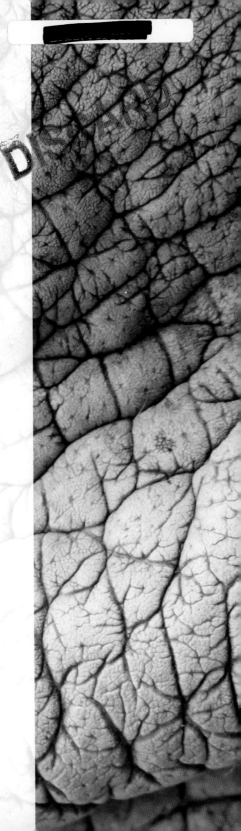

TABLE OF CONTENTS

Hello, rhinoceroses!

Five kinds of rhinoceroses live in Africa and Asia.

Some rhinos live on savannas. Others live in rainforests.

Wrinkly rhinos have soft, thick skin. The skin is brown or gray.

The snout has one or two horns.

A big rhino can move fast!

It charges at threats.

Rhinos eat woody
plants. They push
down trees and dig
up plants to eat.

They find water
to drink.

A calf is a baby
rhino. It stays with
its mother. It learns
how to find food.

Adult rhinos
live alone.

They flick their tails at bugs. They wallow in mud. They rest in shade.

Goodbye, rhinoceroses!

Picture a Rhinoceros

tail

skin

foot

nostril

ears

mouth

horn

eye

Words to Know

rainforests: warm forests that get lots of rain

savannas: grasslands in Africa

snout: the nose and mouth of an animal that sticks out from its face

wallow: to roll in dirt, mud, or water to keep cool and stop bugs from biting

Read More

Bodden, Valerie. *Rhinoceroses.*
Mankato, Minn.: Creative Education, 2013.

Schuetz, Kari. *Rhinoceroses.*
Minneapolis: Bellwether Media, 2012.

Websites

National Geographic Kids: Black Rhinoceros
http://kids.nationalgeographic.com/animals/black
-rhino/#black-rhino-closeup.jpg
Read about black rhinos and watch a video.

San Diego Zoo Kids: Rhinoceros
http://kids.sandiegozoo.org/animals/mammals/rhinoceros
Learn more about the five types of rhinos.

Index